Your Invis

A reference for children and adults a

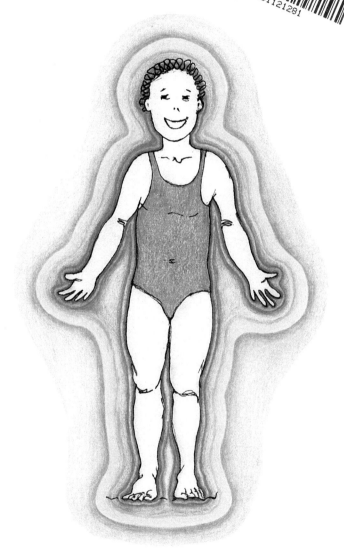

Text by Sharon Montgomery
Illustrated by Cheryl Frederick

Words By Montgomery Publishing

ACKNOWLEDGMENTS

This book would not be possible without the support of several people. To the Healing Touch team (especially Loy and Inger) at Knox United Church in Calgary, thank you for your encouragement and steadfast support. To Heather Faris, ARC practitioner, thank you for the practice and wisdom shown through many sessions. To Cheryl Frederick, artist, thank you so much for grasping the intent of the text and illustrating the book so beautifully. Your drawings convey many levels of wisdom, yet are simple for children to grasp. To the supportive ministers at Knox United, particularly Grant Dawson, who guided me as I tried to simplify and condense centuries of spiritual wisdom into child-sized bites. Knox's three ministers (Grant, Drew and Dan) agreed to my field testing the book with children in the Sunday program. Their valuable feedback to Dan Moulton and me enlivened my Sundays for two months. Drew Strickland enabled sales and presentations in study groups and church events. For literary critiques, thanks to Christopher Wiseman (University of Calgary and Writer-in-Residence for ACWS), Carolyn Pogue (author and peace activist) and Janice Kinch (University of Calgary, Faculty of Nursing). To Gloria Bieber of Life Portraits, thanks for the photographs of my auras and the encouraging reading. To Lexus Bird (participant in the field test group) thank you for your 12-year-old wisdom and careful reading. To my new-found writer friends, especially Carolyn, Lorna and Coral, a huge thanks for helping me promote this book far and wide. To my friends and family, who read various drafts, thank you for trusting me and supporting me on this path. May we continue to describe our discoveries as we journey!

Blessings to us all!

Sharon

FOR THE ADULTS
Introduction

YOUR INVISIBLE BODIES was conceived as a response to yet another course in energy healing. I practised Reiki and Healing Touch for over two decades, but seldom concerned myself with the implications of energy work. I was content to accept healing results as a mystery, far beyond my comprehension. In 2002 I started studying healing treatments with The ARC Institute. ARC stands for "A Return to Consciousness" and is taught by its founder Pietro Abela. ARC combines energy work with dialogue, to access deeper causes of disease. During the first weekend of instruction, Pietro's matter-of-fact explanation of energy fields challenged me to embrace reality rather than mystery. My western-educated mind sought a rational explanation. I felt so uncomfortable with this cognitive dissonance that I wished I had learned about energy fields when I was young. My knowledge about how human beings operated was based on university courses in education and psychology. On the third day of the course, I told Pietro, "What we need is a children's book on this stuff so it's not so hard to accept when we're older." He said, "Good idea."

YOUR INVISIBLE BODIES is my children's book, to help young people understand what it means to be alive. It contains dense information that may challenge as well as inform. The children in the study group had little difficulty with these ideas. They eagerly shared their own experiences about their bodies, feelings, thoughts, and spiritual beliefs. The process also helped me to reflect on my own experiences, seeking universal truths with the children.

YOUR INVISIBLE BODIES is not intended as the final word in understanding spirituality, but as a stepping stone for children. Its teachings provide a place to stand and be supported.

People construct their own beliefs as they grow. Reality depends on personal experience, so there are as many realities as there are people. Based on MY life and MY experience, everything in this book is true.

Part II of this book is a study guide entitled 'For the Adult'. Its questions and activities are designed to assist adults in discussion with children. A reading list for adults is also included at the end of Part II. If used with a group of children, this book can be read and discussed over several (8-14) sessions.

Part I: For the Children

Your Invisible Bodies

Look at yourself in the mirror. What do you see?
You see the outer, visible, parts of yourself. But parts of you are invisible.

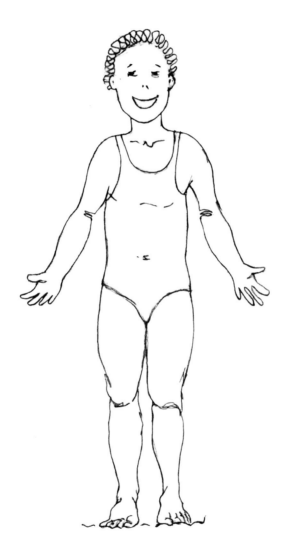

They are part of you, too!
What we see when we look at an object or person is their physical shape
and appearance. But there is so much more to a person.

We have invisible bodies as well as visible bodies. The invisible bodies are connected deep inside us, but spread out beyond our skin. We can't see them because our eyes aren't sensitive enough to receive their energy waves. We have seven bodies that connect inside our body, along a central line. The places where they connect are called chakras (SHA-kruhs). They are located here:

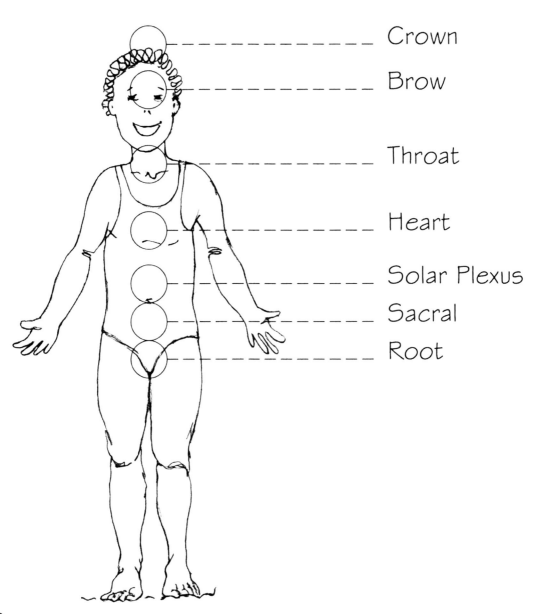

Crown

Brow

Throat

Heart

Solar Plexus

Sacral

Root

The first invisible body spreads about three centimetres (one inch) past the skin. It shows what is happening inside us. This invisible body is sometimes called the etheric (e-THAIR-ik) body. Parts may feel hotter or colder to show what is happening inside. It is connected to the physical body at our private parts, called our root. This body helps us feel connected to our families and first home. When we know we stand on solid ground and feel part of our surroundings, this body grows stronger. The colour frequently used with this chakra is red.

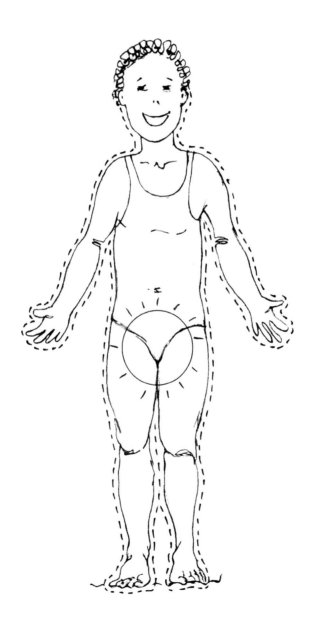

How can you look after your body? You can :

- Eat healthy foods

- Exercise every day to keep the body strong and healthy

- Sleep when tired

- Drink lots of water

- Brush your teeth regularly

- Bathe regularly

- Avoid putting harmful things in the body, like cigarettes, alcohol, drugs

- Avoid dangerous activities that hurt the body or others

- Train carefully when competing in sports

- Go to skilled healers (doctors, nurses, and others) when the body isn't working right

- Be thankful for the body and its health

- Trust what your body tells you

The second invisible body stretches out further, to about 6-8 centimetres (3 inches). It is called the feeling or emotional body. Sometimes people see this body with an orange colour. Our feelings make up this body. It is joined to the physical body below the belly button, in a place sometimes called the sacral (SAY-krul). When we use our energy to create something new, this body grows stronger.

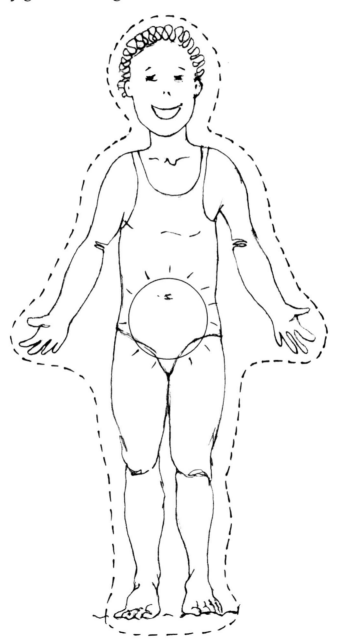

The feeling body decides how the physical body moves and acts. Often, other people can tell how we feel just by looking at us. When someone feels sad his or her body droops down and shows little energy. Angry feelings make the physical body tighten up. Happy feelings make us stand taller and move more easily and gracefully. When we are happy we have more energy. Sometimes we're so happy we even dance for no reason at all, we just want to move!

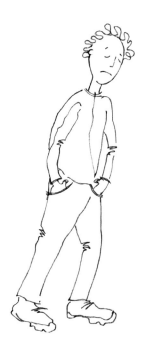 

This emotional body shows everyone how we feel even when we may not say how we are feeling.

Some people, especially young children, can see colours in this body. As we grow older we may not be able to do that as well. One young man told me he saw colours around people until he was five years old. When he asked his friends what colours they saw around another person, they told him he was crazy. He stopped talking about seeing colours and after a while he stopped seeing them. He didn't want anyone to think he was crazy.

How can you look after your feeling part, this emotional body? You can:

- learn to recognize feelings by noticing what your body is doing

- pay attention to these feelings and try to name them

- know that it's normal to feel sad or angry or scared at times

- tell others how you feel as many people don't know how to read body language, and you may not realize how you feel until you talk about it

- share with others both good and bad feelings

- pay attention to sad feelings and just let them be because feelings come and go, and don't last forever

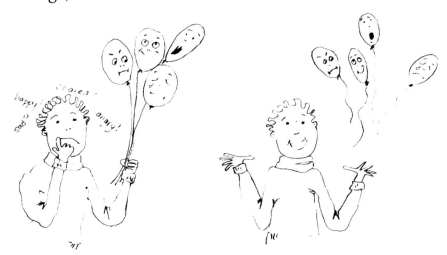

- use your mind to notice what thoughts go with your feelings

- Pay special attention to anger because it means something is wrong. If you release your anger, you will be able to think more clearly about the situation. You may be able to fix what is wrong. If not, try to understand what part belongs to you and what part belongs to someone else.

We have another body that changes how we feel. Around our emotional body is the third invisible one, called the mental body. It spreads out about 10-15 centimetres (6 inches) from the skin. When we think about something, energy flows out to fill this body, giving us more power and space. When a person climbs a hill, he or she sees more of the world than from lower down. In a similar way, when we think about something, we understand it differently than when we use our feeling body. Also, what we feel depends on what we think. We can change how we feel by changing our thoughts.

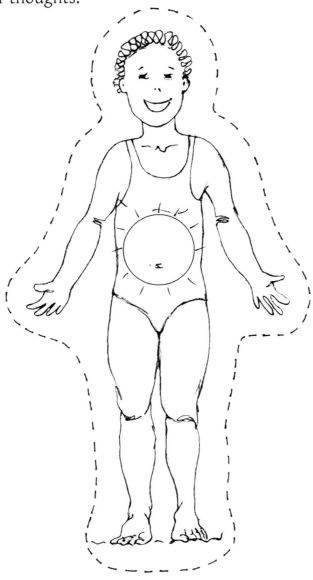

For example, remember a time when your mother left you with a new babysitter. If you thought that she left you because she didn't like you, or because you were being bad, then you may have felt sad.

However, if you thought that she was leaving you to be happy with her friends and you knew she was coming back, you would know you hadn't done anything wrong. You might miss her, but were happier and you would be able to have fun with your new babysitter.

The mental (thinking) body is joined to the physical body below the ribs, in a part called the solar plexus (SO-lur PLEX-us). The color that generally goes with this chakra is yellow. Usually, when you are thinking really hard, your body is still. All your energy is being used by your mind. Thinking is a lot of work. The mind is in the brain inside the head, but also in this mental body. The brain is like the train conductor but the whole mental body is the mind train. We use it all the time, even though we can't see it. The more we use our mind, the stronger this third body becomes.

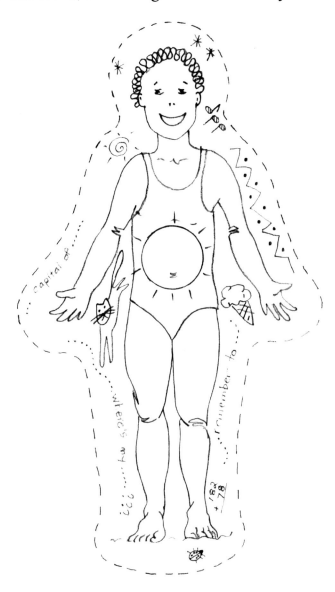

How can you look after your mental body, your thinking part? You can:

- Notice when things don't make sense. Put the problem in your own words. Solve only one problem at a time. Deal with what is in front of you.

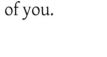

- Remember a time when you lost an item. How did you use your mind to find it? Where did you look? What did you notice?

- Ask questions when you don't understand.

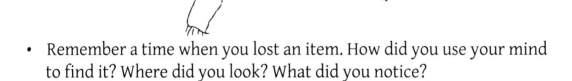

- Give yourself time to make a decision if you feel confused. Don't let yourself be pushed into acting before you are ready.

- Notice what happens when someone is interrupted. The next time you want to interrupt them, you'll know what to expect.

- Notice details of colour, number, shape and use. Notice people and their feelings. Label what you recognize.

- What does this remind you of? Keep an open mind, not deciding too fast. Change your labels as new knowledge comes to you.

- If you are not sure about something, wait for more information before you decide.

- Admit it when you don't know something. It's okay not to know things. Learning takes time and goes on all your life.

Choose what to pay attention to, as some things are harmful. For example, some movies are so scary we can't sleep afterwards. While we may like the thrill of being scared while feeling safe at home, too many scary movies may cause us to believe the world is not safe. When we spend too much time thinking about scary things, we forget the goodness that surrounds us.

The fourth invisible body flows around the first three bodies. It is the spiritual body and stretches 16-30 centimetres (12 inches) out from the skin. Most people think of the spiritual body as a person's soul. It is joined to our physical body near the heart. The colour that usually goes with this body is green. In our heart we may feel love, contentment or sometimes a connection to a bigger world. When this happens, most of us believe we are connecting to something that is outside of us, a power that would exist even if we didn't. For the rest of this book, I will call that something Spirit, but you may call it whatever comforts you. Different names people have called this energy are God, Spirit, Allah, Buddha, Krishna, Goodness, Yahweh, Goddess, Chi, Breath Giver or Love.

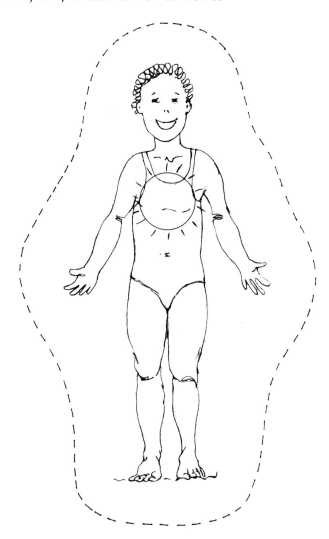

When we pay attention to Spirit, our soul wakes up and reaches out. Sometimes it notices things like beauty or truth or goodness. The soul moves toward what it pays attention to. Many artists and musicians believe that their best music and art comes through this invisible body after connecting with Spirit. The more we connect to Spirit, the stronger our souls become.

If you listen to certain music all the time, you grow in tune with that music. The rhythms and sounds fill all of you, so you move with it. Movies or books can also affect us this way. When we create pictures, make up songs, or write stories, we show others our interests and connections.

Our spiritual body is a part of Spirit inside us. This body is with us from birth. When we were born our spiritual body started as a spark of energy from outside. It is like a star inside, which grows throughout our lives. This star, or light, can never go out, no matter what happens around us. Sometimes it seems small and weak but you can help it grow stronger just by paying attention and imagining its light spreading throughout your body. The spiritual body is our soul, the part that makes us different from everyone else in the world. Each of us is unique, which means one of a kind.

If you find it hard to imagine a star inside yourself, look at this rock, known as a geode. Since stars can exist inside hard objects like rocks, or living fruits like apples, I believe it is possible for stars to be inside people. Geodes and apples can remind us of our inner star.

This geode was photographed at the Mineral and Gem Show in Tucson, AZ in 2008. The stone is about 1 meter high. It is a type of geode called Fairystone, and was found at Abitibi, Quebec.

How can you look after your spiritual body? You can:

- Look for signs of beauty, truth, love, or goodness

- Listen to others who tell you about Spirit, from their own lives or from books or art or events

- Pray or talk to your guiding Spirit, especially when you are troubled

- Listen and notice how your prayers are answered

- Think and feel and act as if you are joined with loving Spirit

- Take time alone to be still so all your parts can feel balanced

- Love, and keep practising love to everyone, not just those whom you like

Imagine someone you care about and send them love.

- Love yourself. If an inner voice tells you that you're wrong or stupid or not good enough, remember that your Soul is meant to be whole and strong and balanced. You ARE special. Don't always listen to that put-down voice because it can be wrong. Another word often used for Soul is Self. Love your Self/Soul as much as you love others.

- Be open to new ideas because no one ever knows all about the universe or how the world of spirit works. We are always learning and discovering more about nature, the universe, and life.

- Forgive others who hurt you, especially if they didn't mean it. To forgive is to let go of hurt, instead of holding onto it.

- When people do bad things on purpose, try to tell them how you feel about what they did.

- If you hold onto hurt and anger for a long time, then your mood can grow ugly, or you could get sick. Think about forgiving the other person so you can be free of bad thoughts and feelings. You might find it helpful to talk with a grown-up at such a time.

- Forgive yourself when you do something wrong. Learn from your experience. No one is perfect all the time. We all make mistakes.

These bodies make up the layers in our aura (OR-rah). The dictionary says the aura is the invisible presence that flows out of living things. A person who is healthy, happy, thoughtful and loving usually has beautiful colours in his or her aura. We may not be able to see the aura, but we can feel it or sense it through our own invisible bodies. Sometimes we don't know why we like a certain person so much, but our invisible bodies move us toward people who offer us what we need to grow. When a person is happy and creative, his or her energy draws others like a magnet.

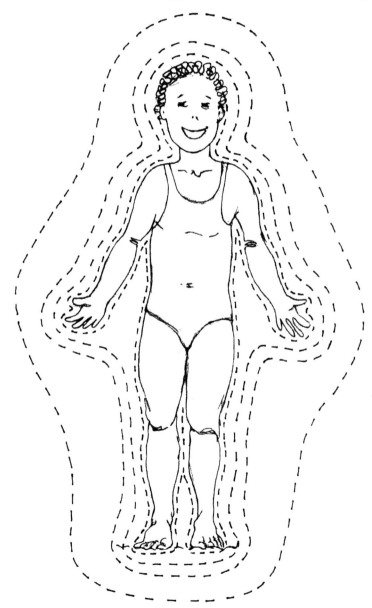

Who is in charge of all these invisible bodies? YOU ARE.

You live in your physical body every moment until you die. Because it's your body YOU are always in charge. The star inside you is the Self or Soul. This is your spiritual body awakened. Sometimes the Self feels big, especially when all your invisible bodies are balanced and working together. Sometimes it feels small. The star is always there and can help you feel more confident. When you are confused, try to relax and notice your breathing. Breathe deeply to send the air to your heart, imagining a golden light filling and wrapping it. This will help your Self be more in charge, as it sends the light throughout your body.

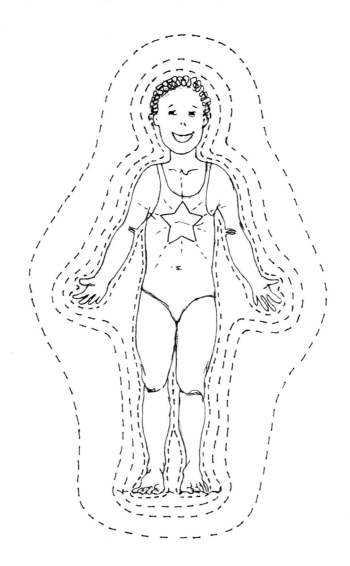

You may find it helpful to be still somewhere private or in nature to know your Self. Many people do that by sitting and paying attention to their breathing. This is called meditation. Try this for five minutes a day and your Self will grow stronger. Then your Self can more easily be in charge of you.

YOU are a whole person and your Self (Soul) is your place of power.

Your Soul knows your feelings, thoughts, and wishes, so when you act with your Self in charge, people will come to know the REAL YOU. You will have more confidence and trust in your decisions. Your Self protects you when you are in danger. (Spirit may be helping you too.) Even when ugly or mean things happen to you, your inner star cannot be hurt. Its light never goes out. The Self grows throughout your life as you experience and learn more. Even when you are old, your Self can still become wiser and stronger. The Self is always YOU, who you really are and who you were meant to be, from birth. It is the most precious part of you.

Some children suffer illness or troubles that could make grown-ups crumble. The stars inside these children often grow very strong very early, to help them survive. They still have hope and they show that hope to others.

The Self is always whole and connected with the rest of you. It's the centre of all your invisible bodies and it connects with Love.

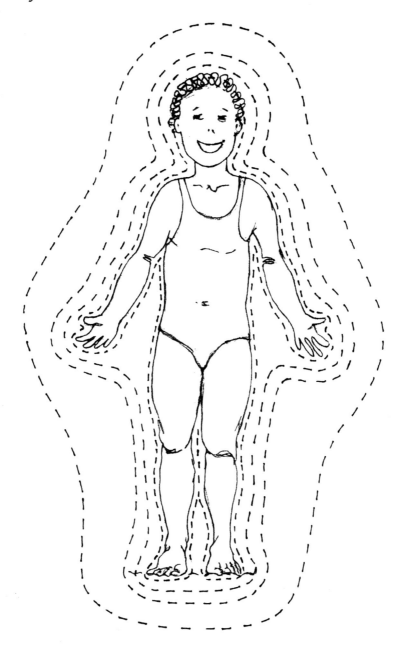

When you die, your physical body can no longer live in this world. Whether accident, illness, or old age, something stops working inside and the physical body dies. Your Self (or Soul) leaves the body and goes home to Love (another name for God, Spirit, Allah, Buddha, Krishna, Goodness, Yahweh, Goddess, Chi, or Breath Giver).

FREQUENTLY ASKED QUESTIONS

Is one of my invisible bodies better than the others?

No, they are all equal to each other and equal in importance. Everything works together, and all parts are necessary.

How do I know this is true?

You can feel your etheric body because it TINGLES, prickles, **SHIVERS** and gives other sensations. Sometimes it makes your hair stand up when you are afraid.

You can feel your heart and spiritual body getting bigger and warmer when you melt into a hug.

You can feel the excitement of the mental body when your mind discovers new ideas.

You can feel peace or excitement in your heart and soul when the spiritual body is connected to Spirit or beauty. Most schools and churches in North America don't teach children about invisible bodies, but some do. Often it is spiritual teachers from different countries and/or earlier times who teach these ideas.

What spiritual leaders have taught about the invisible bodies?

Ancient teachings from India, over 5000 years old, talk about universal energy. Chinese teachers 3000 years ago called this energy Qi (pronounced Chee) and taught the need for balance between opposites. Jewish teachings through the Kabbalah, which is based on much older Egyptian and Babylonian practices, call part of this energy astral light. In Buddhism we find descriptions of energy fields around the human body. These beliefs have shaped the health practices in India, China, Tibet and Japan. Doctors and healers there often use different treatments and techniques than we use in the western world. These methods, like acupuncture or Reiki, are slowly becoming available to people around the entire world. As well, aboriginal people throughout the world have healing practices that work with energy through ritual and symbols.

This Chinese character means Qi, which is the same symbol for Wind. It shows Spirit moving over rice fields. Spirit, as Wind, means we can't see it directly, only what is affected by it. It could also mean Steam Rising from Cooked Rice.

What do today's spiritual leaders say about our invisible bodies?

Some are comfortable with these ideas, some are not. It depends on who you ask.

There are many books that describe how energy works. We can't usually see energy, but we can see what it does, and we may be able to sense it in other ways. Many people now are using energy healing to treat illness and injury.

Did Jesus Christ, who Christians follow, know about these invisible bodies?

He might have, because he was Jewish and understood the idea of the Holy Spirit as a moving wind or force. In fact in Jesus' language, Hebrew, there is only one word for both "wind" and "spirit." The Bible tells how Jesus healed the sick and often said "Do not fear." This shows he knew a person's feelings made a big difference to their health. There is no record of him referring to invisible bodies around a person. Jesus tried to teach people about God, so they would trust God and be happier. Through stories and actions he helped people think differently. He wanted them to be more healthy, loving, and able to live full lives. Jesus treated people as if they were living in their Soul bodies. He acted from a strong centred and balanced Self, as God's partner on earth.

Did the prophet Muhammad, the founder of Islam, know about our invisible bodies?

He might have, because like Jesus, he healed the sick. The Sufi branch of Islam practices spiritual healing, where teachers work on the "inner heart" to heal illness. They believe that when they join with the Divine (Allah), healing energy flows through them to bring another person into wholeness. This is the same belief that modern healers use. Muhammad said you must seek remedies from medicine also, because for whatever disease Allah created in this world, He also created its cure. Muslim healers studied herbs and the natural world to find treatments for disease. They discovered many ways to treat illness which later helped Europeans improve their medical practice.

There is no record in the Koran (the Muslim Holy Book) of Muhammad talking about invisible bodies. However, he strongly believed in the healing spirit of Allah. Muhammad tried to teach people about Allah and how to make strong communities that looked after everyone.

What if I see colours in a person's aura, and no one else around me sees them?

This does not mean you are crazy. At some time you may meet others who also sense energy (as colours or vibrations). Seeing energy is a gift that arrived with your Star inside. Your vision is more sensitive than most peoples'. Trust your own sight and experience. Seeing colours may help you to become a great healer or artist. Whatever it means, accept it and use it to help others. If you want to know what the colours mean, just ask, and the answer will come to you.

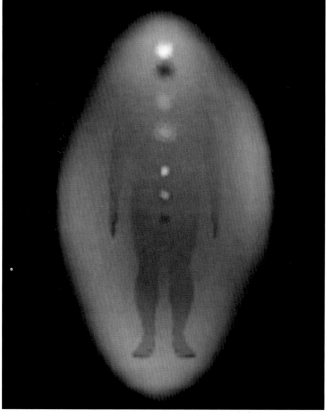

www.lifeportraits.ca

You could talk to your parents or another relative, as this gift often runs in families. They might understand you better if you tell them about the colours you see. You were given this talent for a reason, and it is part of you.

Can I learn to notice the invisible bodies on someone else?

You may become good at sensing or feeling where these invisible bodies are on another person. You might feel different temperatures or thicknesses, or your hands may tingle. That knowledge is what healers use to make people feel better. They can work with invisible bodies to bring them into balance with each other. Then the person feels better in their physical body too.

Should I try to be in touch with all my invisible bodies all the time?

No, just notice which part seems to be in charge at different times. If you don't feel good, then try to connect with your Soul body to bring balance and healing.

If I'm in my soul body, does that mean I'm a good person?

It could. It should mean that what you do is true for your own thoughts, feelings, and beliefs. You will act the same way most of the time. Others will recognize that you are telling the truth about yourself. They will learn to trust you more, which will help you to keep your friends.

Can people still be bad if they are aware of their invisible bodies?

Perhaps. Being good or bad depends on what you do to other people and other living things. You get to decide how to act in the world. You decide what is good for you. If you choose to act in a selfish way, not thinking about how your actions might hurt another, then you could be making a bad choice. Making good or bad choices is part of growing up. Everyone can learn from a bad choice.

If I make a bad choice, does that mean that I'm a bad person?

No, it means you made a bad choice. If you learn from your mistake and don't do it again, then you and others will get over it. Everybody makes different choices. It's part of being human, part of learning and a big part of growing up.

Are these four invisible bodies all the ones we have?

No, there are three more layers, anchored at the throat, forehead, and top of the head. Their colours are blue, purple and white.

What do they do?

They work with the first, second and third bodies as mirrors of them. They show how healthy our bodies are. When you are young, it is enough to know about the first four invisible bodies. The other ones get stronger as you grow older.

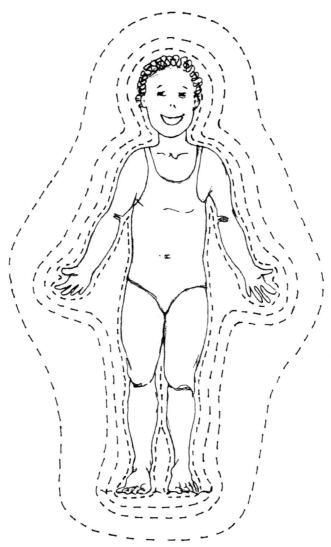

How can I believe this?

For the last two centuries scientists, teachers and healers have explored the energy fields around the human body. Many wrote books about their experiences with this invisible energy. In the last 20 years we have built machines and cameras that are sensitive enough to receive and show these invisible bodies. Russian scientists created a camera (Kirilian) that can recognize a person's aura. Here is a picture of my aura, taken with a camera linked to a computer. At present, some digital cameras are sensitive enough to photograph energy.

www.lifeportraits.ca

My friends don't believe in the spiritual body. Why should I?

Because you can. Once you know this, you can decide if it is true for you. If you honour your inner star (your Self) and Spirit, then life could make more sense to you. You may be happier. You could have more help from the universe. You could have more hope because following your beliefs strengthens your actions. When you live in harmony with your spiritual beliefs (no matter what name you use) your life will be fuller.

Part II: For the Adult

USING THE BOOK WITH A GROUP OF CHILDREN

YOUR INVISIBLE BODIES, written for children aged 8-12, is intended for insightful conversation between adults and children, rather than serving as a book for children to read independently. It provides the opportunity for children to reflect on and share their own experiences. An earlier draft was used with children in the Sunday program at Knox United Church in Calgary, Alberta. These 'field test' children discussed the ideas, asked questions, tried energy exercises, coloured the pictures, and suggested a few changes.

This study guide is based on 10 – 12 sessions of about 40 minutes each. If discussion is animated, it could take longer. If there are more than 10 children, the group should be divided according to age. Gender differences were not relevant in the field test group.

Each session has suggested questions and resources. The facilitator's questions are printed in italics. The pages that list ways to care for our invisible bodies provide many insights that call for examples. Adults are advised to take their time when presenting the concepts, following the lead of the children.

The adult can teach through sharing his/her own story, particularly of events and feelings experienced at the students' age. If the children do not offer examples of their experiences, the facilitator should model the conversation. In the event of co-facilitators, their dialogue will inform the children.

A useful guideline is that the children talk at least half the time. Consider "How many of the children are actively engaged in this topic for how much of the time?" If they are not engaged, move on to the next topic and grab their interest. Modify the activities according to their age and ability. If the children lose interest, find out why and adapt with shorter simpler questions, real life examples, and movement activities. You may need to repeat some of the energy exercises given in Session 1.

The older children generally follow the conversation eagerly, but consideration must be given to the youngest ones. Also, a quiet child could be encouraged at times to "hold the space" with hands extended, sending love to the rest of the group. In this way they can feel like active participants without saying anything.

The children could be given opportunities to colour the pictures. This would slow down their conversation, enabling the ideas to be absorbed. Colouring and conversation contribute to the child's comprehension of the sometimes dense information. As children colour simple drawings, the reader must pause, giving children time to better reflect on and remember the content. In this way, the child may take more ownership of the book and its ideas. Each child will take his or her book home at the end of the study.

Resources

One book per child
Nesting (Babushka) dolls or boxes
A geode, and/or an apple

Session One: Our Physical Body (Cover – p. 4)

Show the book cover. *What do you predict this book will be about?* Record their ideas on a chart, to refer back to at the end of the study.

Page 1: *When you look at yourself in the mirror what do you see?* Accept all answers equally. *What do you think are your invisible parts?*

Energy Exercise: Rub hands together. Then hold hands apart, with palms facing each other. *Can you feel energy between your hands? If so, slowly move your hands apart until you no longer feel the energy.* Compare the distances, and assure them that people feel energy in different ways. *What do you think this energy is?* Accept all answers, guiding them to personal energy like electricity, made by each person. Don't insist on one right answer.

Energy Exercise: Have each child in turn sit quietly with eyes closed. Explain that you will be moving your hand toward his/her body, and when s/he feels it enter her/his energy field, to say "Now." Ask the child to say where s/he feels the hand approaching. Open eyes to notice how far your hand is from the physical body, and if it is in the area described. *How do you think you knew that?* Accept all answers. (Alternatively, have them do this in partners, depending on the size of the group.)

Page 2: Read together. *Have any of you heard of these before?* Assure them they are real.

Page 3: Read together. Have the children place their hands near their body, to discover if they can feel their own energy fields. *Move your hands outward to sense changes in your invisible bodies. What did you notice?* They may sense changes in density, temperature, an apparent 'edge', or shift. They also may not sense any changes at all.

Page 4: Before turning the page, ask *How can you look after your body?*
Record their answers on a chart or whiteboard. Read p. 4 together, comparing the lists.

Session Two: Our Emotional Body (p. 5-7)

Show Babushka dolls (sometimes called nesting dolls) and have each child take apart one layer of the doll, then pass it onto the next child. *This is an example of different layers, but all one doll. We have layers inside us, and layers outside us. We may not see the layers, but we can feel or sense them.*

(Alternatively, use nesting boxes.)

Page 5 - 6: Read together. *Do you believe that the emotional body shows others how we feel? Let's find out.*

Feeling Exercise: Pass around an envelope containing slips of paper, each labelled with a feeling. (Suggestions: angry, confused, sad, surprised, happy, afraid, embarrassed, nervous, excited, shy, brave, curious.) *Each of you will take one piece of paper, read it, but don't show your word to anyone else. Then, when it is your turn, show us that feeling with your body. The rest of us will guess the emotion that you are showing.* Allow at least ten minutes for this exercise, and encourage questions and responses.

Page 7: Read together. *Have any of you ever seen colours or shimmering around someone's body?* Explain that this is unusual but okay. *What would you do if someone told you they saw colours around you?*

Session Three: Caring for Our Emotional Body (p. 8)

Review. *What do you remember about the feeling body?*

How can you look after your feeling part, this emotional body?

Write down their ideas on a chart or whiteboard.

Page 8: Read together, pausing after each statement to ask them to share particular examples from their own experience. General questions to move the discussion:

Is it easy for you to talk about your feelings?
Who do you talk with most easily about your feelings?
What makes it easier to share your feelings?
Do you need someone else to ask you how you are feeling?
Do you ever ask others how they are feeling? If not, why not?

How do you feel about this session?
What have you learned from listening to each other?
Do you feel closer to each other?
How do you show good feelings?

Elicit ideas about smiling, relaxing the body, moving closer, perhaps touching one another, giving a hug.

Move the children toward understanding that in some families, people don't talk about their feelings (especially the bad feelings). Most people are more comfortable talking about their activities than their feelings. That needs to be respected. However, often all it takes is for one person to ask, *How are you feeling?* When one person answers, others start talking about how they feel. If you get a one-word answer, ask *Why do you feel that way?* You will learn more about them and usually will feel closer to them. *With whom in your family would you feel comfortable asking how they felt?*

Talking about feelings is hard, and learning how to do it well goes on all our lives.

Session Four: Our Mental Body (p. 9-13)

Review what they have learned about the invisible bodies so far.

Page 9: Read paragraph. *Do you have an example from your own lives of how changing your thoughts changed how you felt?*

If not, move to page 10. Read. *Does this make sense?* If not, use an example from your own life to illustrate the statement.

Page 11: Read together. Look at the examples of interests within the mental field. *What would be in your mental body?*
How can you look after your mental body, your thinking part?

Record responses, but if none, then turn to p. 12 - 13 and read the examples. *Has this happened to you?* Share their stories.

Some people learn best by what they see, and others learn best by what they hear. Still others learn best by what they do, or what they feel inside. What is your favourite way to learn?

Explain that most people have two favourite ways to learn, and if the children can't name their favourite, ask them how they most easily learn new information, through pictures, by reading and writing, by listening and speaking, or by doing something? *If something doesn't make sense to you, use your favourite way of learning to better understand it.*

Page 13: Read together. *What thoughts scare you? What can you do to stop or change your thinking about that?* Move them toward seeing possibilities for acting, to prevent the scary events from occurring. You may have to share a specific example from your own life if they are stuck.

Session Five: Our Spiritual Body (p. 14 – 18)

Review what they recall from the previous session.

Page 14: Read together.

Which of these names works best for you?
Do you have other names you prefer to use?
Do you get a picture in your mind with your preferred word? How does that help you?

Page 15: Read together. *Does this make sense to you? What do you notice in her energy field? What would be in your spiritual energy field?*

Page 16: Read together. *Does this make sense to you?*

Show a geode, with the cut crystal side hidden. *What do you think is inside?* After predictions, turn it over to show the crystalline structure inside. Pass it around for each child to hold. The geode will illustrate the star inside rocks.

If no geode is available, show an ordinary rock. *What do you think is inside this rock?* After predictions, look at the photograph which follows. Read together.

A second example is an apple. *Do you think there could be a star inside an apple?* Cut it across the middle, then turn the two halves to show the core in the shape of a star. Later, you can cut the apple into pieces for the children.

Since there are rocks with stars or crystals inside, and apples with stars inside, don't you think there would easily be a star inside a person? The geode and the apple remind us of beauty inside, even though we may rarely see it.

Page 17: This page has a picture of the Fairystone Geode, found in Abitibi, Quebec.

Page 18: *How can you look after your spiritual body?*
    Read the statements together. *What fits for you?*
    What is your soul interested in?

Page 19: Read statements. *What fits for you? Who can describe a time when you experienced this? What was happening around you then?*

Session Six: (p. 19-22)

Page 20-21 : Read together. Practice breathing deeply and imagining a golden light filling your body. Take five minutes to experience this. *Do you feel any different from before we practiced that?*

Page 22: Read together. *Can you remember a time when you did not behave with your true Self in charge? Why do you think that happened?* Ensure them that everyone has many experiences of pretending, usually when we are trying to control a strong feeling. It is normal, and relaxing into your Self takes practice.

Page 23: Read together.

Do you know any children with serious illnesses?

How do they show hope to others?

If no examples emerge, ask *What about children who face serious problems? What are they?*

Be mindful that serious is relative, and whatever the children offer is true for them. The emphasis is on how hope is shown to others.

If the children with the problems do not have hope, ask *What hope can you offer when the problem is talked about? Where does hope come from?*

Move toward 'believing that you are not alone and that a greater power than the individual is available'. Move them toward understanding that listening to someone shows they are not alone. When you ask a person to tell you their problem, if you then don't really listen or care about them, they will feel hopeless, not hopeful.

If their problem is too big for you to help, go with them to someone who can help. For example, if a friend is being bullied, go together to talk to a responsible adult.

Session Seven: Death, (p. 23)

Page 24: Read together.

Take all the time you need to hear their stories about death. Some may have lost grandparents, pets, relatives or friends. Model how to be present when people deal with grief. Have tissues present.

Use drawing paper and crayons for them to show their feelings about death and/or afterlife.

Everyone feels loss at times in their lives. This is part of being human.

It's good to express your sadness in tears, or art, whatever helps you. ... Grief doesn't last forever.

It may seem that the tears will never stop, but they will, because we can only cry long enough until something shifts inside, then we stop. .... We may cry again another time, but each time it eases up.

Grief doesn't last forever, but if you don't express it, the feelings stay locked inside your body and may cause illness.

Share your grief with a good listener. They don't need to know what to say, or offer advice.

When the children have had enough time to share their personal stories, ask:

What ideas about an afterlife have you learned from books or movies or TV?
What ideas have brought you comfort?
Could different ideas all have a bit of truth to them?
What is the most important truth in your idea? Lead them to the concept 'We are not alone.'

Session: Frequently Asked Questions (FAQ) (pp. 25-35)

What questions do you have about your invisible bodies? Record on chart or whiteboard.

Answer the questions they raise, especially if they are not represented on p. 24-30. Trust yourself and reflect your own beliefs and faith.

Turn to FAQ (starting on p. 25) and progress according to the children's interest.

Page 25: Read together. Discuss statements as the children desire.

Page 26: Read together. *What do you know about any of these beliefs? Do you know anyone who has received an acupuncture treatment? Describe it as clearly as you understand.*

Look at the traditional Chinese character for Qi. *How is Spirit the same as Wind?*

Page 27: Read. *Have you ever had a healing treatment? What was it like?*

Activity: Form partners, and have each person give and receive energy sweeps while seated on a chair. One person sits with feet flat on the floor, eyes closed, hands in lap. The partner stands behind them and sweeps hands about a hand-width off the body, starting above the head, past the shoulders and down to the hips. Repeat 3 times. Then move to the front of the person and sweep from head to toes in long gentle strokes. Repeat 3 times. Then stroke from knees to the feet, and rest hands on the top of the feet, to complete the treatment and ground the seated person. Exchange places. At conclusion, share what you experienced. Allow at least ten minutes for this exercise.

Session: Jesus Christ (p. 28)

Read together.

What else do you know about Jesus?

Accept all responses. If you are uncomfortable with any of their statements, express your ideas respectfully and truthfully. Try to give examples to illustrate your thoughts, rather than abstractions. Be mindful of the cognitive development of the children and don't overwhelm them. If you have a favourite parable that explains your truth, it will be easier for them to grasp the meaning. Less is more.

Depending on their responses, you may be able to continue to p. 29 in this session.

Session: Muhammad (p. 29)

Read.

Do all spiritual leaders have to be the same?

What is the same about Muhammad as about Jesus?

If someone else believes differently than you do, does that mean that one of you is wrong?

How do you know what is true for you?

Do you believe it possible that people of different beliefs can live peacefully beside each other? What would it take for that to happen?

Session: Sensing Energy (pp. 30-31)

Read p. 30 together.

What do you think of this picture?
How can seeing colours be a talent?
What are your talents to use?

How could members of a family help each other, if one or all sense energy?

Repeat the exercise from the first session, where we felt the energy when we rubbed our hands, then pulled them apart. *Does this experience feel different from the first session?*

Read p. 31 together.

Remember the feeling of energy in our hands the first session.

Would any of you like to become a healer?
Who do you know who helps others feel better?
How can you help others feel better?

Session: Good and Bad Choices (p. 32)

Read together.

How can you tell who is good or bad? Lead them toward basing judgements on behaviour, not other attributes.

If your friend makes bad choices, do you remain friends? Why or why not?
What else could you do?
If someone in your family makes bad choices, and you have to live together,
what can you do?

It may be helpful to refer to page 8 about expressing feelings. This session could continue indefinitely. Try to wrap up with each member knowing one action he or she could take in this situation.

Session: Photographing Energy (pp. 33-34)

Read pp. 33-34. Look at the picture of the author on the back cover. Verify that this is a real person. Respond to the statements and photograph.

Session: Conclusion (p. 35)

Read together.

Do you believe in the spiritual body?

When is it easiest to believe?

When is it hardest to believe in the spiritual body?

How can you remind yourself of Spirit when it is hard?

Lead toward reciting a prayer, imagining your place of meditation, feeling the golden light within, remembering a time when you felt totally loved, or another strong emotional connection.

Close with a prayer of thanks, with each person saying what they are grateful for. For yourself, celebrate gratitude with the children. Your expression of gratitude will be more mature than theirs, and can guide them to greater appreciation of relationship with each other and with Spirit. Hugs and/or other expressions of respect and caring (eg. Namaste) would be appropriate too!

ADULT READING LIST

Ballentine, R. Radical Healing: Integrating the world's great therapeutic traditions to create a new transformative medicine. Harmony Books. New York, NY. 1999

Bartlett, R. Matrix Energetics: the science and art of transformation. Atria Books. New York, NY. 2007

Brennan, B.A. Hands of Light: A guide to healing through the human energy field. Bantam Books, New York, NY. 1998.

Carroll, L & Tober, J. The Indigo Children: the new kids have arrived. Hay House Inc., Carlsbad, CA. 1999

Fillmore, Charles. Christian Healing. Unity School of Christianity. Unity Village, MO. 1975

Graham, R., Litt, F. & Irwin, W. Healing From the Heart: A guide to Christian healing for individuals and groups. Wood Lake Books. Kelowna, BC. 1998.

Hay, L.L. You Can Heal Your Life. Hay House, Santa Monica, CA. 1984.

Joy, W.B. Joy's Way: a map for the transformational journey. An introduction to the potentials for healing with body energies. J.P. Tarcher, Inc. Los Angeles, CA. 1979

Ledwith, M. & Heinemann, K. The Orb Project. Atria Books, Simon & Shuster. 2007

Mate, G. When the Body Says No: The cost of hidden stress. Alfred A. Knopf. Division of Random House. Toronto, ON. 2003

Myss, C. Anatomy of the Spirit: The seven stages of power and healing. Three Rivers Press. New York, NY. 1996

Myss, C. Why People Don't Heal and How They Can. Three Rivers Press. New York, NY. 1997

Stein, D. All Women are Healers: a comprehensive guide to natural healing. The Crossing Press. Freedom, CA. 1990

Wauters, A. Chakras and Their Archetypes: uniting energy awareness and spiritual growth. The Crossing Press. Freedom, CA. 1997

Zukav, G. & Francis, L. The Heart of the Soul: emotional awareness. Free Press. New York, NY. 2001

Sharon Montgomery is a former teacher and guidance counsellor who writes plays, songs, and articles. Sharon has practised Reiki and Healing Touch for 25 years, and more recently, healing therapies through The ARC Institute (A Return To Consciousness). She wrote this book in order to present contemporary knowledge of human energy to children. This book is Sharon's way of explaining a small part of the mystery she has experienced during her spiritual and healing journey.

Cheryl Frederick graduated with a Diploma of Fine Art from the Alberta College of Art and with a Bachelor of Education from the University of Calgary. She has a continued passion for reading and learning, as well as an expanding interest in creating spiritual connectedness with others. Cheryl was invited to enliven the text of this book through a mutual friend and Healing Touch practitioner, which Sharon considers divine intervention. Her drawings capture the essence of the text, making it understandable even to young children.